Holiday Magic Books

April Fools' Day
MAGIC

by James W. Baker
pictures by George Overlie

Lerner Publications Company ⌐ Minneapolis

To my friend and fellow magician, K. Bhagynathan, who could fool me not only in April but throughout the year. The stage presence and magical showmanship he exhibited served as an inspiration to me.

Library of Congress Cataloging-in-Publication Data

Baker, James W., 1926-
  April Fools' Day magic.

  (Holiday magic books)
  Summary: Describes how to perform magic tricks with
April Fools' Day as a theme.
  1. Tricks—Juvenile literature. 2. April Fools'
Day—Juvenile literature. [1. Magic tricks. 2. April
Fools' Day] I. Overlie, George, ill. II. Baker
James W., 1926-   Holiday magic books. III. Title.
GV1548.B325 1989   793.8   88-24451
ISBN 0-8225-2230-6 (lib. bdg.)

Manufactured in the United States of America

2   3   4   5   6   7   8   9   10   99   98   97   96   95   94   93   92   91   90

CONTENTS

INTRODUCTION

When a magician accidentally pours milk into his top hat, he gets a soggy hat... but wait... and read the tricks in this book... his hat is not even wet! April Fool!

On the first day of April — April Fools' Day — men and women, girls and boys play absurd but good-natured jokes on each other. Those who are tricked are called "April fools."

When you perform magic tricks on April Fools' Day, your friends will be entertained and amused, even as they are tricked. You will make April fools out of your friends, but they will have as much fun being fooled as you will have fooling them.

APRIL FOOL AGAIN

HOW IT LOOKS

You show three pieces of construction paper—one red, one green, and one yellow—to the audience. Put all three pieces into an empty paper bag. Remove the red piece and then the yellow one. Ask a volunteer which color is left in the bag. When she says "green," you remove a piece of pink paper with "APRIL FOOL" printed on it. Of course, the volunteer will ask you to turn the pink paper around, thinking that it is green on the other side. You turn it around to show that the other side is also pink and says "APRIL FOOL AGAIN." Then show the audience that the bag is empty.

8

1. You will need three cards made of construction paper, each about 5 x 8 inches (13 x 20 cm). One is yellow and another is pink. Print "APRIL FOOL" on one side and "APRIL FOOL AGAIN" on the other side of the pink card. For the "fake" card, paste a piece of green paper to a piece of red paper at an angle (**Figure 1**) and trim.

2. You will also need a large paper bag with the top rolled down so that you can see into it.

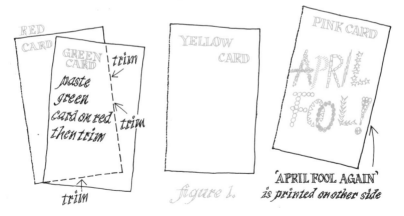

RED CARD

GREEN CARD trim

paste green card on red then trim trim

trim

YELLOW CARD

PINK CARD

APRIL FOOL!

figure 1.

'APRIL FOOL AGAIN' *is printed on other side*

9

1. Before you begin, fan out the cards. First is the "fake" card with the red and green parts showing. Next is the yellow card (**Figure 2**). The pink card is hidden behind the "fake" card.

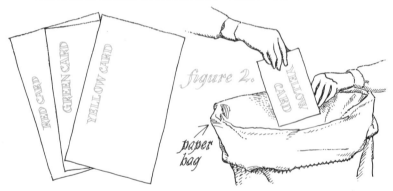

figure 2.

RED CARD
GREEN CARD
YELLOW CARD
YELLOW CARD

paper bag

2. Show the fan of cards to the audience, saying that you have three cards, one red, one green and one yellow. Pick up the paper bag with your other hand, show that it is empty, and put it back on the table. Close up the fan of cards and drop them into the bag.

10

3. Reach into the bag and bring out the "fake" card so the audience only sees the solid red side. Lay it on the table, "fake" (red and green) side down. Reach into the bag, bring out the yellow card, and lay it on top of the red card.

4. Ask a volunteer from the audience which card is still in the bag. She will say "green."

5. Reach into the bag and bring out the pink card so the words "APRIL FOOL" face the audience. When the volunteer tells you to turn that card over, you show that the other side is also pink and says "APRIL FOOL AGAIN." Then show the empty bag to the audience.

HOW IT LOOKS

Give your friend a math problem to do and tell
her that a banana will predict her answer. She
will probably think you are crazy. Nevertheless,
she does the math problem and her answer is 5.
When she peels the banana she discovers it has
already been cut into five pieces inside the skin.
The joke is on her.

HOW TO MAKE IT

1. To prepare the banana, poke a needle into its skin and carefully push it through until you feel it hit the skin on the other side.

2. Pull the needle out a little and gently move it back and forth, pivoting it, without enlarging the tiny hole it made in the banana skin. It will slice through the soft banana (**Figure 1**).

3. Do this to the banana in four places to cut the banana into five pieces inside the skin.

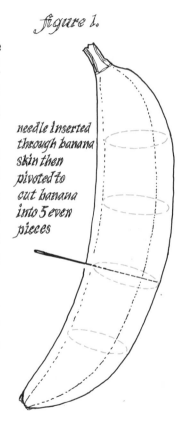

figure 1.

needle inserted through banana skin then pivoted to cut banana into 5 even pieces

4. Gently rub your finger over the four holes made by the needle and they will barely be visible.

HOW TO DO IT

1. Tell your friend to choose a number without telling you what it is.

2. Have her add to it the next highest number. Then have her add 9, divide the answer by 2, and subtract the original number. Her final answer will always be 5. For example:

Your friend chooses a number . . .	418
Adds the next highest number . .	+ 419
	837
Adds 9	+ 9
Divides by 2	846 ÷ 2 = 423
And subtracts her original number	− 418
To get her final answer	5

3. After she has done the math, hand her the unpeeled banana and tell her the banana will reveal her answer.

4. Watch the expression on her face when she peels the banana and sees that it is cut into five pieces.

cross section of banana

tiny hole in banana skin

HOW IT LOOKS

Using nine cards and a special dealing system, you proceed to spell the names of the cards as they turn up. You do it correctly, but when your friend spells and deals the same way he always turns up a joker—the April Fool card.

HOW TO MAKE IT

You will need nine cards of one suit and a joker. Ahead of time arrange the cards facedown, as follows, from top to bottom:

3-5-ace-7-9-2-joker-8-6-4.

16

HOW TO DO IT

1. Holding the cards facedown, tell your friend something like, "I am going to spell the names of the cards. For each letter, I will take a card from the top of the pack and place it on the bottom of the pack. As I say the last letter, I will turn over the card I have spelled."

2. Now you show your friend what you mean. Begin to spell A-C-E. Take the top card and place it on the bottom..."A." Do the same with the second card..."C." With the third card, say "E" and turn up the ace, placing it on the table.

3. Do the same as you spell T-W-O. As you say "O," place the card faceup on the table next to the ace. It will be the 2.

4. Explain once more, spelling T-H-R-E-E. Place the 3 on the table faceup. Hand the remaining pack of cards to your friend.

5. Tell him how simple it is and ask him to spell F-O-U-R. As he is putting cards under the deck one at a time you spell aloud with him—F-O-U-R —and tell him to turn up the last card. Instead of the 4, it will be the joker. Tell your friend that you do not think he followed your directions because he got the joker instead of the 4. Take the pack of cards back and put the joker *on top of the pack*. Spell again, putting the joker on the bottom of the pack as the first letter of F-O-U-R. Turn over the card as you say "R," and it will be the 4.

6. Hand the deck back to your friend and ask him to spell F-I-V-E. When he does, once again he will turn up the joker. Place the Joker back *on top* each time it turns up. Take the cards in your hands again and spell F-I-V-E, which is correct again.

7. Ask your friend to spell S-I-X ("an easy one") but again he turns up a joker instead of a 6. Begin to show your "impatience" and you spell S-I-X, which turns up the 6.

8. Tell him you will show him again with the 7. You spell S-E-V-E-N and turn up the 7.

9. Tell your friend that certainly he must know the system now. Ask him to spell E-I-G-H-T and again he turns up a joker. You look exasperated and ask someone else to spell 8. They do it correctly.

10. Turn to your friend and say something like, "There are only two cards left. Please try to spell N-I-N-E right this time." When he spells N-I-N-E and turns up the last card it is once again the joker. Take the two cards back from him and say, "No, you spell N-I-N-E like this." Spell N-I-N-E and lay the 9 face up on the table. All that is left in your hand is the joker.

11. Hand the joker to your friend, and say: "Since you seem to like this foolish joker so much, take it, and let it remind you of when you saw a magic trick called 'An April Fool Joker.'"

Although the steps may sound complicated, they really are not. Practice this with the cards in your hands and you will see how easy it is to remember the steps.

A SOGGY HAT

HOW IT LOOKS

You show the audience a top hat and a paper cup.
Put the cup in the hat and then take it out. Then
"accidentally" pour some milk into the hat rather
than the cup. But when you put the cup back in
the hat it fills up with milk. You take the cup of
milk out and the hat is not even wet. A sign inside
the hat says "APRIL FOOL."

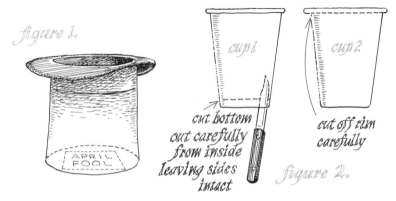

figure 1.

cup 1

cut bottom
out carefully
from inside
leaving sides
intact

cup 2

cut off rim
carefully

figure 2.

HOW TO MAKE IT

1. For this trick, you will need a hat with a flat top that is deep enough to hide a paper cup inside. Print "APRIL FOOL" on an index card and tape it to the inside of the top of the hat (**Figure 1**).

2. Prepare two of the same, solid-color, paper cups by cutting the bottom out of one and cutting the rim off the top of the other (**Figure 2**). Nest the bottomless cup inside the rimless cup so they appear to be one cup (**Figure 3**).

3. You will also need a pitcher of milk.

22

figure 3.

bottomless cup

rimless cup

1. Put the hat upside down on the table and place the cup—actually the nested cups that look like a single cup—in the hat.

2. Look as though you are puzzled. Take only the inner cup—the bottomless one with the rim—back out of the hat and place it on the table. Do not let the audience see the missing bottom or the rimless cup remaining in the hat.

3. Pick up the pitcher of milk and act like you cannot make up your mind whether to pour it into the cup on the table or into the hat.

4. Begin pouring the milk into the hat. Actually, you pour it into the rimless cup which you have left in the hat unknown to the audience.

5. Act worried and say something like "Oops! I think I made a mistake. I should have poured the milk into the cup."

6. Pick up the bottomless cup from the table and carefully place it into the cup with the milk in it inside the hat.

7. Wiggle your fingers over the hat. Then reach into the hat and take out the cup—really the two nested cups—containing the milk. Pour the milk back into the pitcher.

8. Pick up the hat to show that it is dry and let the audience see the card that says "APRIL FOOL."

A FOOLISH SHIRT

HOW IT LOOKS

Select a volunteer from the audience who is wearing a sweater over a long-sleeve shirt. Unbutton the cuffs and collar button of his shirt. Grasp the collar behind his head and pull the shirt up and off over his head without disturbing his sweater.

HOW TO MAKE IT

The volunteer is really a *confederate*, or secret assistant, but the audience does not know it. He must prepare for the trick ahead of time like this:

A. Drape his shirt over his back like a cape without putting his arms through the sleeves.

B. Button the top two buttons of his shirt around his neck.

C. Button the cuffs of his shirt around his wrists.

D. Put his sweater on and sit in the audience.

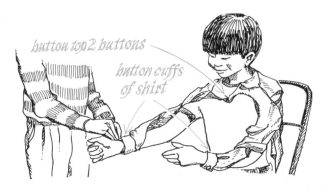

button top 2 buttons

button cuffs of shirt

HOW TO DO IT

1. Ask for a volunteer from the audience and choose your confederate.

2. Have him sit in a chair in front of the audience. Unbutton the top two buttons of his shirt and the buttons on his cuffs. Tell him you are doing this because he looks like he is too warm.

3. Reach behind his neck, grasp his shirt collar, and pull his shirt completely off over his head.

ICE IN APRIL

HOW IT LOOKS

Challenge your friend to lift an ice cube out of a bowl of water with a string without touching the ice, the water, or the bowl. She will probably try to loop the string under or around the slippery cube. When she fails, you show her how to do it and say "April Fool."

28

For this trick you will need a bowl of cold water, an ice cube, a piece of string about 8 inches (20 cm) long, some salt, and a spoon. Keep the salt and the spoon out of sight at the beginning of the trick.

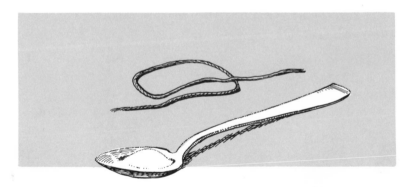

HOW TO DO IT

1. After your friend tries to lift the ice cube out of the bowl, you dip the string into the water to get it soaking wet. Drape one end of the string across the top of the ice cube.

2. Bring out the salt and the spoon and sprinkle a spoonful of salt on the top of the ice cube and the portion of the string on the ice cube.

3. When the salt hits the ice cube, it will melt the ice a little and then the ice will refreeze to form a strong bond with the string.

4. After a few minutes, pull on the string to lift the ice cube from the bowl of water. Say "April Fool" to your friend.

A FOOL'S CARD

HOW IT LOOKS

One volunteer from the audience chooses a card and puts it in her pocket without showing it to anyone. You give a picture of an "April Fool" with holes for eyes to a second volunteer. The second one looks through the eyes of the "April Fool" at the pocket of the first volunteer and announces the name of the card the first one chose. The first volunteer removes the card from her pocket and the second volunteer is proven correct.

On a piece of cardboard about 8 x 10 inches (20 x 25 cm), draw the silliest face you can. Cut holes where you drew the eyes (**Figure 1**). Under the face, write "An April Fool." On the back of the cardboard, just above the eye holes, write "6 of spades." You will also need a deck of cards.

figure 1.

6 OF SPADES

eye holes

AN APRIL FOOL

front of card

back of card

1. First you must "force" the first volunteer to choose the 6 of spades:

A. Have the 6 of spades on the bottom of the deck. Ask the first volunteer to cut the deck of cards at any point and set the top half on the table next to the bottom half.

B. You pick up the bottom half of the deck and place it crossways on top of the other half (**Figure 2**). As you do this, distract the audience for an instant by saying something like, "Have you ever seen April Fool magic before?"

figure 2.

← *bottom half of deck*

C. Now pick up the top half of the deck. Show the card on the bottom of the top half only to the first volunteer, but not to the audience, as you say something like, "Here is the card you cut to," the 6 of spades (**Figure 3**). Tell her to put the card she "chose" in her pocket. You will have "forced" the 6 of spades.

figure 3.

2. Show the silly "April Fool" face to the audience but do not show them the back of the cardboard. Hand the cardboard to the second volunteer. Ask him to look through the holes in the eyes at the first person's pocket to see if he can tell what card she chose. As he moves the cardboard toward his face, he will see that "6 of spades" is written just above the eye holes. Naturally he will go along with you and say "the 6 of spades."

3. Have the first person remove the card from her pocket and show it to the audience. It is indeed the 6 of spades.

HOW IT LOOKS

After your friend chooses a card, you tell her that you have already placed a duplicate of that same card in your shirt pocket. When you begin to remove the duplicate card, you appear to have goofed up the trick but—with a comical turn of events—you turn out to be correct after all.

1. You will need a regular deck of cards and a 9 of hearts from an old deck.
2. Cut the 9 of hearts so that five hearts show on the face of the card (**Figure 1**).
3. You will also need to be wearing a shirt with a pocket. Place the cut card in your shirt pocket, facing out with the cut side down, so no one can see the card.

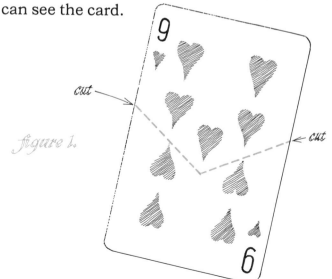

figure 1.

37

1. Bring out the deck of cards and, like the trick before, "force" your friend to choose the 5 of hearts:

A. Have the 5 of hearts on the top of the deck. Ask your friend to cut the deck of cards at any point and set the top half on the table next to the bottom half.

B. You pick up the bottom half of the deck and place it crossways on top of the other half (**Figure 2**). As you do this, distract your friend for an instant by saying something like, "On April Fools' Day, I'm always afraid something will go wrong with my magic."

figure 2.

5 of hearts →

→ place bottom half on top

C. Now you pick up the top half of the deck. Ask your friend to pick up the "card she cut to," the 5 of hearts, which is on top of the half deck lying on the table (**Figure 3**). You will have "forced" the 5 of hearts.

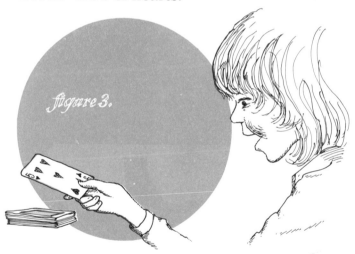

figure 3.

2. Tell your friend that even though she freely chose a card, you had placed a duplicate of it in your pocket ahead of time.

3. Slide the cut card out of your shirt pocket, but only enough to show the first two rows of hearts and the number 9 in the corner of the card. Be sure not to cover the 9 on the card with your finger or thumb.

4. When your friend sees the 9 of hearts, she will tell you that you are wrong. You tell her you are never wrong and ask her what card she chose.

5. She will say she chose the 5 of hearts. You say that is what you have and pull the cut card out of your pocket, dropping it on the table. Tell your friend that if she does not believe you, she can count the hearts on the cut card herself.

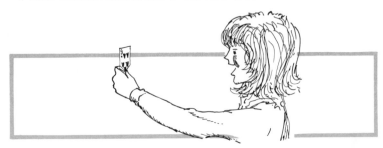

APRIL FOOLS' BETS

Here are some bets you can make with your friends on April Fools' Day, knowing you will never lose:

1. Bet your friend you can drop a cardboard match onto a table and make it land on its edge.
Secret: Bend the match in half and drop it from about one foot (30 cm) above the table; it will land on its edge.

2. Bet your strongest friend he cannot hold a glass of water on the palm of his hand with his arm extended straight out for seven minutes.
Secret: It cannot be done, even by the strongest person.

41

3. Bet someone you can balance an egg on its end on a table.

Secret: You must put a small mound of salt under the tablecloth on the table ahead of time. You balance the egg on its end by pressing it down into the little mound of salt under the tablecloth.

4. Bet a friend that if you place a sheet of newspaper on the floor and both of you stand on it, he still will not be able to touch you.

Secret: Place the newspaper on the floor in a doorway, close the door, and tell him to try to touch you.

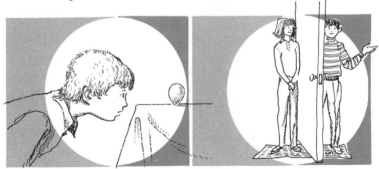

5. Tell your friend that if she can tear a sheet of paper into four equal parts, you will give her a quarter.

Secret: When she successfully tears the paper into four equal parts, you hand her one of the pieces—a quarter of the sheet.

6. Bet your friend that she cannot bend over and pick a pencil up off the floor if she stands with the back of her legs and heels against the wall.

Secret: Her position against the wall makes it impossible to bend over and pick up the pencil without losing her balance and falling over.

7. Bet your friend that there is a spot where he can stand and not be able to lift his foot.

Secret: Have your friend stand with his head, left shoulder, left side, and left foot tight against a wall. Then tell him to lift his right foot off the floor without moving any part of his body away from the wall. It cannot be done.

8. Tell your friend that you have two coins in your closed fist and their total value is 35 cents although one coin is not a dime. Can he tell you what the two coins are?

Secret: You have a quarter and a dime. Remember, you said *one coin is not a dime*. That is true. One coin is a quarter. The other is a dime.

9. Tell your friend that you can tell the color of a crayon simply by *feeling* it. Have her hand you a crayon behind your back. You then tell her its color.

Secret: While the crayon is behind your back, rub your right thumbnail against the tip of the crayon, getting a tiny piece of crayon under the nail. Hold the crayon in your left hand and bring your right hand to your brow as you go into deep concentration. You can then see the color of the crayon under your finger nail.

10. Bet someone he cannot find a single numeral —words do not count—on any United States coin other than in the dates.

Secret: There are none.

TRICKS FOR BETTER MAGIC

Here are some simple rules you should keep in mind while learning to perform the tricks in this book.

1. Read the entire trick several times until you thoroughly understand it.
2. Practice the trick alone or in front of a mirror until you feel comfortable doing the trick, then present it to an audience.
3. Learn to perform one trick perfectly before moving on to another trick. It is better to perform one trick well than a half dozen poorly.
4. Work on your "presentation." Make up special "patter" (what you say while doing a trick) that is funny and entertaining. Even the simplest trick becomes magical when it is properly presented.
5. Choose tricks that suit you and your personality. Some tricks will work better for you than others.

Stick with these. *Every* trick is not meant to be performed by *every* magician.

6. Feel free to experiment and change a trick to suit you and your unique personality so that you are more comfortable presenting it.

7. Never reveal the secret of the trick. Your audience will respect you much more if you do not explain the trick. When asked how you did a trick, simply say "by magic."

8. Never repeat a trick for the same audience. If you do, you will have lost the element of surprise and your audience will probably figure out how you did it the second time around.

9. Take your magic seriously, but not yourself. Have fun with magic and your audience will have fun along with you.

ABOUT THE AUTHOR

James W. Baker, a magician for over 30 years, has performed as "Mister Mystic" in hospitals, orphanages, and schools around the world. He is a member of the International Brotherhood of Magicians and the Society of American Magicians, and is author of *Illusions Illustrated*, a magic book for young performers.

From 1951 to 1963, Baker was a reporter for *The Richmond (VA) News Leader*. From 1963 to 1983, he was an editor with the U.S. Information Agency, living in Washington, D.C., India, Turkey, Pakistan, the Philippines, and Tunisia, and traveling in 50 other countries. Today Baker and his wife, Elaine, live in Williamsburg, Virginia, where he performs magic and writes for the local newspaper, *The Virginia Gazette*.

ABOUT THE ARTIST

George Overlie is a talented artist who has illustrated numerous books. Born in the small town of Rose Creek, Minnesota, Overlie graduated from the New York Phoenix School of Design and began his career as a layout artist. He soon turned to book illustration and proved his skill and versatility in this demanding field. For Overlie, fantasy, illusion, and magic are all facets of illustration and have made doing the Holiday Magic books a real delight.